Look:

Love Letters

poems by

Maxx Dempsey

Finishing Line Press
Georgetown, Kentucky

Look:

Love Letters

ACKNOWLEDGMENTS

I want to thank my family for raising me up, and friends for the
unconditional support during this process. Chelsea, you have been with me
since the very first word. This one's for you.

Publisher: Leah Huete de Maines
Editor: Christen Kincaid
Cover Art: Maxx Dempsey
Author Photo: Chelsea Rosevelt Dennis
Cover Design: Elizabeth Maines McCleavy

Order online: www.finishinglinepress.com
also available on amazon.com

Author inquiries and mail orders:
Finishing Line Press
PO Box 1626
Georgetown, Kentucky 40324
USA

Contents

A purpose of human life, no matter who is controlling it, is to love whoever is around to be loved.

—*Kurt Vonnegut*

Portrait

A small rock is thrown high into the air. It is craggy and gray. Just a hunk of concrete, really, not sedimentary, not igneous, just some gunk mixed with unassuming pebbles. It is easily gripped in a hand and tossed upward. The chances of injury are slim, but not impossible. Of course, if a head, if my head, is at the other end of its trajectory, damage could be done. After it hits (no injuries reported!) things are calm. The rock just lies there. It could be sleeping. It could be watching something inane on its phone. It could be putting off changing the cat litter boxes. It could be thinking of escape, like out of a hatch in the side of a satellite. That shining efficient satellite, comfortable in its orbit, solar panels instead of arms. Miles up there—easy ride. Nothing in its path; space clear in all directions.

Wake

Death makes the grown fall to the pavement. I have seen this. Rye distilled offers an allowed amplification of this great grief. It allows the starched church shirts to be shed. It allows Uncle Kevin the relief of driveway gravel, and the sobbing shaking his shoulders like a jackhammer. Someone shoots off fireworks in the back of my grandmother's small yard. They explode in the sky, bombs of colored sparks. I don't see them. I am searching the ground, listening for the quakes of the falling. My Aunt Karen, the youngest child, brings me, the youngest child, into the bedroom my mother shared with her sister when they were young. She says, *your Uncle Bobby loved you very much,* and tucks the rough blankets around me, beer stale on her breath. She kisses my cheek. She leaves the hall light on and the door open. The low yellow light makes the angles grow sharp on the statue of Mary in the hall. From downstairs the noise booms. I stay awake, eyes on the statue, begging her not to crumble. Death makes the grown fall to the pavement. I have done this. I am finally struck by the acute illness of missing. I crash onto my knees and say, please. My grandmother, grieving wife and then grieving mother, uncovers casseroles and tidies ashtrays. My mother, grieving sister and then grieving daughter, uncovers a section of my grandmother's closet devoted to black. The oldest now, I uncover lawnmowers and take out the trash. I put on his shoes in a rush to find mine and I am that child again. I am searching the ground. I am listening.

Fourth of July Outside of Buick City

Four exit ramps down from
Flint's jagged city edge on the
Fourth of July, amidst lawn
chairs and dusty hoods of cars
lined up, my uncle makes his
rounds to each niece, nephew,
daughter, son, to light sparklers
and watch us make our names
appear out of smoke. I sit on the
front of his Buick that we all
know he wrenched out of sheet
metal with his bare hands. *Don't
blink and you'll see the blue ones,*
he tells me. He points his rough
finger at the sky. *They come fast
and you'll almost always miss
them, just don't blink.* He drives
my sister and me back to
Grandma's at the end of the
night. I sink into the midnight
blue of his back seat, nestled like
a racoon, tired eyes still searching
the sky.

After the Desert

My grandmother called my mother a vagabond. I thought she wore that title with pride until she put on a crucifix again after I left for college, after the divorce. She had followed him to Arizona. To wide earth. Saguaros and Peyote buttons. There were no cathedrals in that open space. On Sundays she collected arrowheads in the desert, untethered from the taste of thin wafers. When I was born she cut her hair. She began picking at her thumb. All the way down to the first knuckle skin was scraped away. She sat quietly in the green chair sculpting it into something she could recognize. I was a barely bottled bundle of broken currents, a flame of her former self. She sat and picked and watched me, knowing she had passed me something dangerous on my way into this world.

Corson Auditorium with Low Light

We ran up two flights of stairs as
if just released into the wild. We
fell to the landing, clunky and
unrehearsed. Warm velvet carpet,
all sound tempered by dampened
walls. We were two birds rising as
one movement. This was our
secret, not the kiss, but our flight
into a crimson nest. And my
hurricane met her late summer
again and again. Do I even have a
molecule of love in me? And now
the oak tree outside has waged
war on my house. An acorn
caught me on the arm and left
a bruise the size of a quarter. I,
too, wreck havoc when the wind
blows. I relinquish control of
my limbs and think little of my
targets. I have no eyes for the
marks I leave.

Rachelle, Rachelle

Once the dirty mailbox, middle number missing, and the deep two track often muddy driveway is teased out of the brambles and cattails, the path taken winds through rusty Cadillacs and refrigerators without doors. She is waiting on the small wooden porch and we walk to our spot; two rusted barrels truncated and fashioned into a bench. I feel the pull of cast-off tires and a life of wrenching on rusted cars, sifting through piles of scrap for the metal recyclers. We smoke ditch weed grown from castoff seeds. We avoid her mother, a thin ghost with an almost empty bottle of Mad Dog in her hand. We play Alice and Chains and she talks about boys. There are brothers around, I barely notice. We find our own bottle. We take tentative sips. We pass it back and forth. She licks her lips after each drink. My eyes follow her tongue. The music from the tape deck eases to a stop. My mother's car horn sounds staccato through the air.

Mom, You Should Have Gone to California.

I am three generations broken. Mother; death came to your father first, then your marriage died, and you watched my lover almost kill me. I married a sharp taste in the back of my throat because she didn't turn her head when I tried to kiss her. Who's potatoes did you piss on, oh great ancestors of mine? Who cursed our soil? And mom, in college you met a man who wanted to take you west. Do you still feel that tidal pull? My father is now happy in love. He has no memory of the house falling down around us; silent dinners and silverware scraping plates. Pill bottles blowing me kisses from the cupboard.

And Then, Prague

We find the lake on a paper map and
take the bus past the square Soviet
buildings, past the Astronomical
Clock, even past the beer stands,
lines of overalled workers drinking
the first pint of the day. We strip to
our underwear and wade into warm
water churned by thick drops. This
pond is our dirty little secret we
make clean with our baptism. The
boys across the way are riding BMX
bikes. They are catapulting off a
wooden ramp into the water. They
arch their bodies back and perform
miracles of physics into the deep.
They don't see our own arched
bodies, our own miracle.

Driving on Tryon Road

She says, *I don't want to hit myself*, and grinds her fist into her chest in a circle. I ask her to take my hand and squeeze as hard as she can. She is rocking back and forth and her nose is leaking and there are tears on her cheeks. She is screaming as if being torn apart from the inside. Ahead a long stoplight changes to red. I am thinking of the cars freely driving past us, how they are flowing like a herd of deer out of a burning forest. She is trying to birth herself as a child who will be loved with the fierceness of one who has not been loved. I am her midwife bearing witness to this miracle. I speak in a low and even voice. I don't say much, just the words you say to a labor-weary mother and the coos you make to the wailing just-born.

This Man

He asks me if there is something wrong with his eyes. He tells me he would never hurt me. This man's daddy was a preacher. This man preaches Jesus in crowded shopping malls. We pray together, in Jesus name, let us pray. Alone with him in his room, the door shut behind me, I am looking for anything I could use as a weapon. This man tells me every Christian has 3900 angels around them at all times. He asks me if there is something wrong with his eyes. I ask him to watch my finger, I move it back and forth and his eyes follow. This man, who is leaning over me, this man, blanketed by angels, his eyes are alright. They are blue with yellow around the center. They are small for his face. They are shaped like mustard seeds.

Daniel

Belly laughs, us doubled-over, spilling espresso and over-pulling the shots. Me; *barista with a heart of gold,* you always said, sneaking my hand into the tip jar. I spent every stolen moment out back sucking cigarettes. Or in the bathroom unfolding cellophane, rolling up dirty receipts with hands stained brown. At night we locked the doors and you taught me what words not to say while we shouted along with Biggie, Hov and Ye and took turns mopping the floor. We talked broken hearts while taking out the trash. We crammed anything that could fit into the brief moments between customers, for which you had contempt, and who would never know. For years I watched you bounce around the back bar joking and teasing until we all felt like kin. You, forever wisecracking, grinding it out on the assembly line—I didn't think I was worth a better gig, you didn't bother to try. We hated every single shift. And then we stayed. And I got clean. And then I left. Did you make it back to Boone? Daniel, make it back to Boone. Read Vonnegut and write stories in the mountains. I'm pleading with you, finish your mixed tape, find a club and set up your equipment in the back. Find love. Soothe yourself. Read these words one day and know what you taught me about which hearts glitter.

I Play Basketball

I launch into lay-ups, I return from the net, I make baskets, plenty of baskets. My mind is somewhere thinking about her or I'm not sure, I'm not listening, I'm stretching and my body is moving—it's unremarkable, it's just happening. I play basketball and it is autumn. The court is packed-earth. I am thirteen again—playing alone on the broken cement of old Central school. Breath I can almost see—sweat on the nape of my neck—I am moving and stretching and not listening; Glorious not to be listening—no hook! My hands are real on the ball. I play basketball on an uneven court and I have not twisted an ankle—the dull thunk of my dribble—the pounding of the backboard—the slicing through the net. My breath, accordion rhythm. The placement of my real hands on the stippled ball—bent knees, the in-breath, the jump—

South Bend, Indiana
September, 2001

Inside the hotel room we play a
game of rugby with Gideon's
bible. We throw it hard against
the hollow walls. Merrill grins
while winding up. We hit with
pillows stripped of angel-wing
casings. We jump from bed to
bed. The Good Book's spine
now cracked and broken, open
to Ecclesiastes, staying that way.
Seth sits cross-legged on the now
bare mattress. He cradles the
book with both hands, *and this is
vanity*, he reads. The brown stain
on the mattress around him
creates a halo.

My poetry teacher gives us an
assignment the morning classes
resume. *Imagine you are on the
plane. She says. Imagine you are
in the building or watching from
the street. Imagine you are the
plane.*

And this, too, is vanity.

Landscape

The sky is big and the clouds are so red they are the heart of this earth. I drive the same damn road, but this morning fog hangs in a stand of trees right there across the highway. The sun rises behind it, and my God it is an orangish red orb and I stare right at it. *This is the shape of our sun*, I think. And yes, the loggers are taking the trees, but there are still enough. I have been asleep for years. I am waking up now. Like an animatronic robot I shake into being when I receive something shiny. Like you, shiny thing, come closer. And this poem is not about you. It's just, you should see it this morning, warm vermillion light diffused by mist, scattered by spruce standing like fence posts holding back another world wanting to pulse into this one. In this world maybe I don't drive to work. In this world maybe I drive to your house. Maybe you get in the car and we drive due east.

Kick

The wall of windows facing north overlooks the shallow stream dressed in a river's cloak. Cedar sweepers line the banks. In their branches spiders cast long strands into the air like kite strings. Inside the house I trace the bluebird on my great-aunt's metal bed frame. Grandmother's quilt is a blanket of slate on top of me. Sheets are wrapped around my limbs like a tent catapillar's nest. There is no sleep. And on my way home, too early, the car tries to steer itself back. I wrestle it along the snaking shore of Lake Michigan. I am pulling it back towards the gray streets and I fall into them like a knife thrown into a bucket of putty. At night, in bed next to a sleeping lover who is slowly catching on, I am stoned but awake. I crawl out on a branch, my web unfurling.

Baptism at Jordan Lake

I made my way barefoot down a rocky path and did not stop walking when I reached the shore. The rising sun reflected scarlet off the water. It could have been a lake of fire. Nothing looked different when I came up—No charred earth, no paradise. The lake was amoebic and still. The empty two-lane caressed its curves. If she would come I'd bring her down to the banks. I would show her what it feels like to break through the surface not caring if it is water or flame. I would ask, do I seem different to you now?

Ian

During the worst of it I was in a closet buffered by clothing. Socks—a multitude of socks. Baskets of folded sweatpants and old t-shirts. The wind roared constantly. Gusts bent trees to the earth where they shook in a bowing dance. I waited for a limb through the window. Our shattered shared futures tethered together. It would be broken beams and cats scattered, I was sure. In the quiet calm after the terror I stood sheepish in a yard that looked almost the same as the morning before. And there were lives lost in Florida. Boats flung from the sea, smashed houses. The ocean is cold and final. In my house the worst didn't happen. Instead it was just eight hours of a held breath, a prayer held between my teeth. To the tree it's just a lost war against gravity, a deal made with the Fates as a sapling, an acquiescence to the gale. To the gust it's just the mundane pulling of a weed. And we, collectors of things sacred to only ourselves, are no match for this plan. We set ourselves against the blows and they come anyway. And safe behind the billow the stars twinkle on and off. They dodge our wishes by disappearing from sight for our one urgent moment.

Jeanie

Your presence here still permeates the soil. It is in the delicate and the hardy offerings you left behind. I know your tan arms cradled bundles of bulbs, your knees were made dark by the earth. When we moved your mattress it revealed two serrated kitchen knives. What ghosts did you see when the blossoms you tended folded back into themselves? Here, on this land, there are your obvious gifts, Japanese maples, Mimosas. A Crape Myrtle burning bright with fuschia pyramids. There are blueberry bushes so lush they buckle. And there are surprises, like Dog Fennel. I wrestle the meaty stalks, the fairy forked leaves brushing my sweat and dirt streaked face, until I learn the quiet purpose: A natural tick repellent. The reason why not one biting threat latches to my skin even as I stand shin-deep in St. Augustine grass. They are tall and proud sentinels holding back the wild. And you, dear thing, shivering in winter, your compound of Eden quiet and wrapped in a chain link fence. Your offerings bent under frost and the slight snow of tentative North Carolina coldness. Were you frightened by the neighbors ten acres over? Did you leave your light on deep into the night and fight the darkness, vines slow-crawling into the house through its cracks? When we arrived, the multitude of grasses had gone to seed. The vines of Kudzu had taken over. When I finally get around to tending the wildness, each dead limb I wrench away reveals pockets of flowers, too many to name. You traded your carefully coaxed field of pretty things for the safety of concrete and stone. A paradise to uncover outside. Inside, a legacy of exile.

Wood Cat

The vet said she is just a wood cat, this tiny orange side-swirled bundle found up a tree. I picture her forming from a seedling, or protruding out of the side of an oak like a burl. When I found her she was covered in fleas, her belly looked like the inside of a dragon fruit. The squirming parasites gave her a fever and she lay on my chest all night, legs splayed. Her small sweet potato body moved up and down with each of my in-and-out breaths. I hoped she thought she was a part of me. And just like any child who is a wild and unpredictable beast, this recovered kitten would drive a stray claw into my thumb in a moment of play. Over three days I watched the puncture wound flare up into an angry red dome and grow like a blister. In the examination room, the doctor asked about my little fireball, my dangerous stray. *Ran off into the woods*, I said. I went home and held her little body like a secret.

I Saw a Black Snake

I saw a black snake today and believe me when I tell you it was four feet long. We both startled, me and the black snake, and I want you to see it: It flipped and turned suddenly when it saw me and almost fell over, if it could without legs. Its belly was as black as its top and it was one long curving exclamation. Then it humped over a tree root and rushed off under the brush. In the moments before I moved my legs up under me and exclaimed, the black snake and I were doing exactly the things that we do if we are a human relaxing and a black snake hunting. There was me in my chair under the tall oak, soaking up diffused light through the leaves, the snake meandering along, darting tongue its happy guide. Then I saw it and I spoke to no one when I yelled, *it's a black snake!* And I tell you this now because it is my gift to you; our shared blessing of language-my offering of a framed scene.

One Week Out

*"I am subject to death, I am not exempt from death.
I must be parted and separated from everyone
and everything dear and agreeable to me."*
AN 5:57

The peepers are at it again. Even so, I regard it
as silence. Is this what it's like? Maybe the dead
are alive right next to the living. Maybe they
wake up, dress in pants, a shirt, socks. Maybe
they still slide to the side of the walkway to let
me pass like a gentleman does. He wouldn't
want me to write a poem. He would want me
to sneak a pill and a beer, gulp them both on the
back porch in the dark, listen to ZZ Top and
play darts until 1am on a weeknight. He's gone,
and still, the peepers. The shrill bug sound I
cannot place. the darkness scattered by the
moon. And now, in the house he has left
behind, the molding is still piled by the
fireplace. The tools are wrapped up, separated
by me for him, just before he was gone. The
hole in the ceiling, patched, then patched
again. The air conditioning patched, then
patched again. The mistakes and missteps in
this house are now only stories—what we have
left. Remembrances of strewn screws.

Maxx Dempsey was born a month late in the middle of Michigan's Lower Peninsula. They grew up playing with sticks and climbing trees, and then listening to music and staring out of car windows. They attended Western Michigan University and graduated with a dual-major BA in Creative Writing and Environmental Studies. In 2004 they attended the Prague Summer Program, and wrote during the day and explored the old city at night. Maxx moved to North Carolina in 2012, and has been working and writing there ever since. You can find more of Maxx's published poetry in *The Potomac Review*.

www.ingramcontent.com/pod-product-compliance
Lightning Source LLC
Chambersburg PA
CBHW022106080426
42734CB00009B/1498